LEARN to DRAW!

I WANT TO DRAW HORSES

DAVID CROSSMEISTER

PowerKiDS press
New York

Published in 2019 by The Rosen Publishing Group, Inc.
29 East 21st Street, New York, NY 10010

Editor: Jennifer Lombardo
Book Design: Tanya Dellaccio

Photo Credits: front cover, back cover, pp. 1, 3–24 Chiociolla/Shutterstock.com; cover (horse) Marie Charouzova/Shutterstock.com; p. 5 (pencil and sharpener) KET-SMM/Shutterstock.com; p. 5 (boy) Shyamalamuralinath/Shutterstock.com; p. 6 Janusz Pienkowski/Shutterstock.com; p. 8 mariait/Shutterstock.com; p. 10 horsemen/Shutterstock.com; p. 12 jacotakepics/Shutterstock.com; p. 14 Anaite/Shutterstock.com; pp. 16, 18 Olga_i/Shutterstock.com; p. 20 Vera Zinkova/Shutterstock.com.

Cataloging-in-Publication Data

Names: Crossmeister, David.
Title: I want to draw horses / David Crossmeister.
Description: New York : PowerKids Press, 2019. | Series: Learn to draw! | Includes glossary and index.
Identifiers: LCCN ISBN 9781508167921 (pbk.) | ISBN 9781508167907 (library bound) | ISBN 9781508167938 (6 pack)
Subjects: LCSH: Horses in art–Juvenile literature. | Drawing–Technique–Juvenile literature.
Classification: LCC NC783.8.H65 C767 2019 | DDC 743.6'96655–dc23

Manufactured in the United States of America

CPSIA Compliance Information: Batch CS18PK: For Further Information contact Rosen Publishing, New York, New York at 1-800-237-9932

CONTENTS

Getting Started 4
Drawing the Przewalski's Horse 6
Drawing the Mustang....... 8
Drawing the Shire 10
Drawing the Quarter Horse. 12
Drawing the Thoroughbred . 14
Drawing the Appaloosa 16
Drawing the Arabian 18
Drawing the Shetland Pony 20
Drawing Terms 22
Glossary 23
Index 24
Websites 24

GETTING STARTED

Horses have long been an important part of human societies. In the past and present, they have been used as farm animals. They are also used to pull carriages and sleighs, run in races, and work as service animals to help people with special needs. They make great pets, if you are prepared to care for one. It's a lot of work taking care of horses!

Most horses today are **domesticated**. That means they have **adapted** to being around people over the years to work for and serve them. Very few wild horses are left on the planet today. You might think drawing horses is hard, but it isn't!

In this book, you will learn how to draw eight types of horses. This first one is Przewalski's horse. This horse is a distant relative of modern-day, domesticated horses, and is the last truly wild horse on Earth!

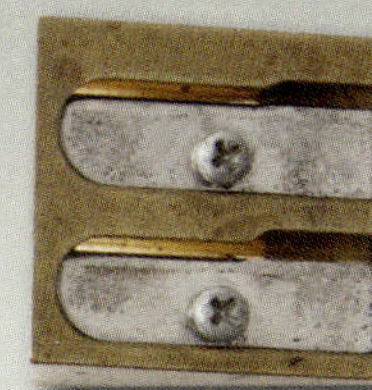

To start drawing horses, you will need a few supplies. You need a sketch pad, pencils, an eraser, and a pencil sharpener.

DRAWING THE PRZEWALSKI'S HORSE

In 1881, a Russian army officer named Nikolai Przewalski discovered and described wild horses he found in Mongolia, which is a country in Asia. The horse was named after him. It's sometimes called the Asiatic wild horse or Mongolian wild horse. Przewalski's horses are generally smaller than domesticated horses. They have a stocky body, a large head, and short legs.

This **species** of horse is in danger of dying out due to the actions of people. Zoos have helped keep this species alive. In 1992, scientists reintroduced 16 Przewalski's horses back into their natural habitat in Mongolia. Today, there are hundreds of them in the wild.

Przewalski's horse was named after the explorer who discovered them. This name can be pronounced puhr-zhuh-VAHL-skee or shuh-VAHL-skee.

1 Draw a beanlike shape for the body of the Przewalski's horse.

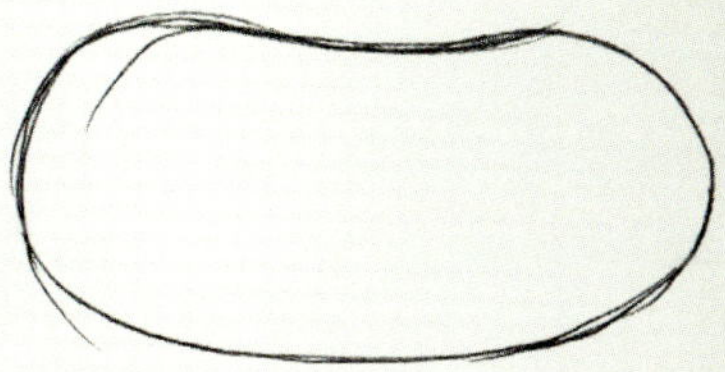

2 Draw a small oval for the head. Notice how much smaller this oval is, and where it is placed on the page compared to the first shape.

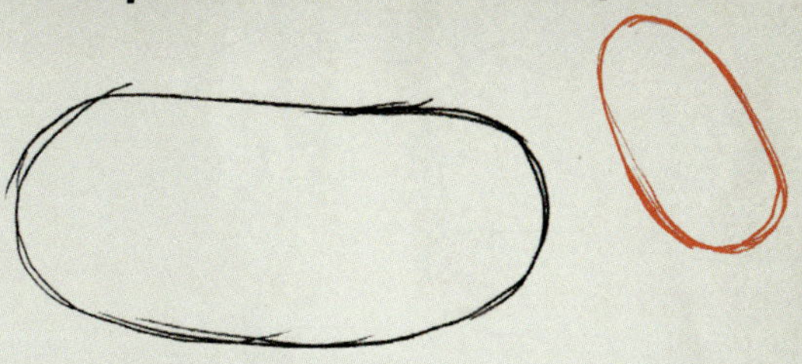

3 Now connect the shapes with two curved lines to draw the neck.

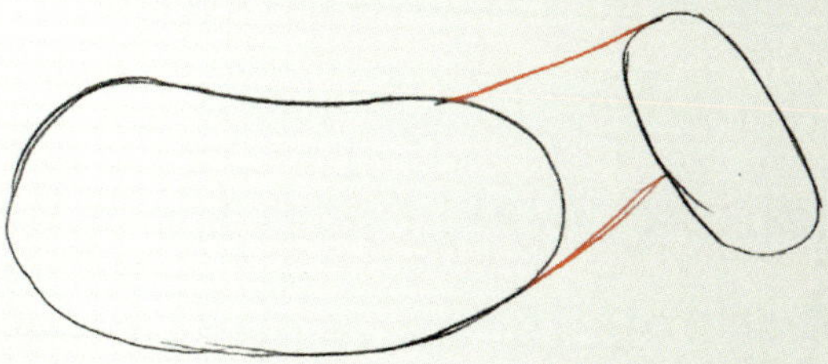

4 To add one set of front and back legs, draw three circles for each leg. Draw two sets of curved lines as shown to join each set of circles. Connect these lines at the bottom with straight lines.

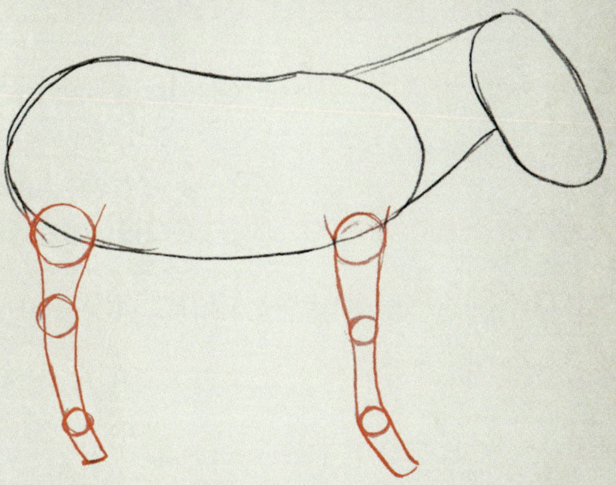

5 Follow the same directions as in Step 4 for the other legs by drawing circles and connecting them. Draw the jaw, ear, eye, nostril, and mouth as shown.

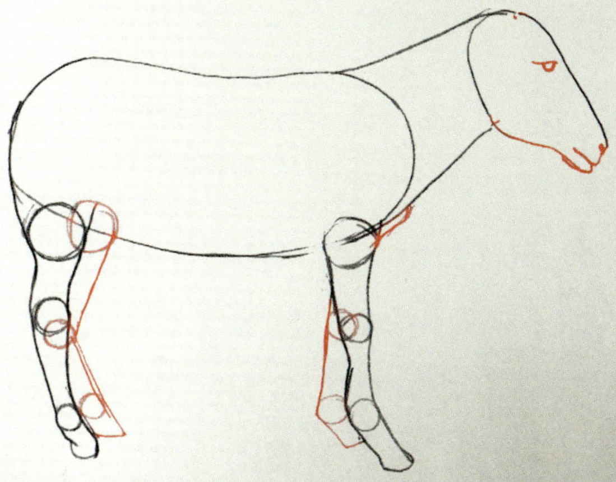

6 Erase any extra lines. Now draw the basic shapes of the tail and mane. The Przewalski's horse's mane is shorter then most horses' manes. Shade in the mane and tail using the side of your pencil instead of the point.

DRAWING THE MUSTANG

When Spanish **conquistadores** arrived in North America in the sixteenth century, they brought horses with them. Eventually, herds of mustangs could be found running wild in the north. They roamed in large groups across the Great Plains.

Ranchers and cowboys called these wild horses broncos. They captured mustangs and trained them. Mustangs were **crossbred** with other horses to make strong workhorses for pulling wagons and **stagecoaches**. Wild mustangs were hunted for their meat in the 20th century, and their populations decreased greatly. In 1971, Congress passed a law that protects wild mustangs from hunters.

Domesticated horses that turn wild, such as the wild mustangs of North America, are called feral horses. They aren't considered true wild horses like the Przewalski's horse.

1 Draw an oval for the body of the mustang.

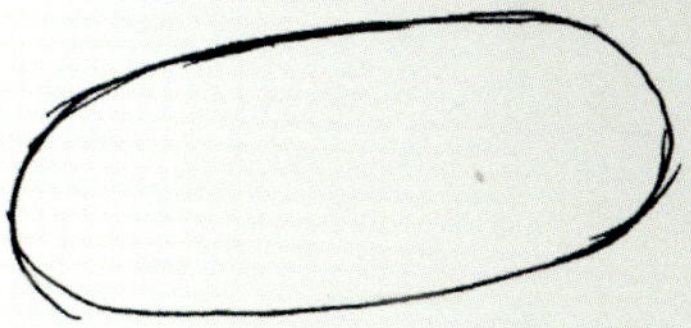

2 Draw a smaller oval for the head. Notice the size of this smaller oval and that it is placed above and to the left of the first oval.

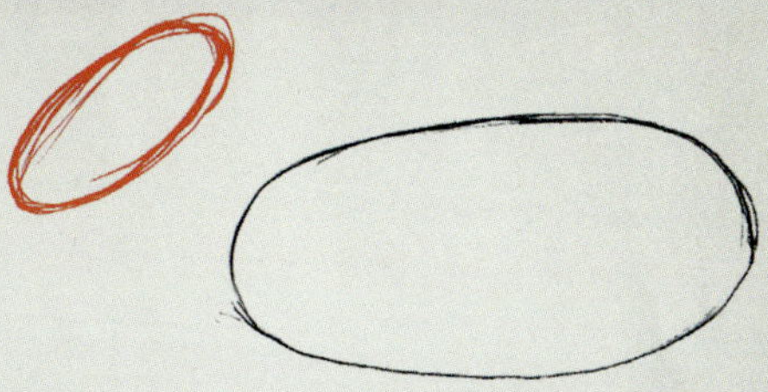

3 Next, to add the neck, connect the ovals with two straight lines as shown.

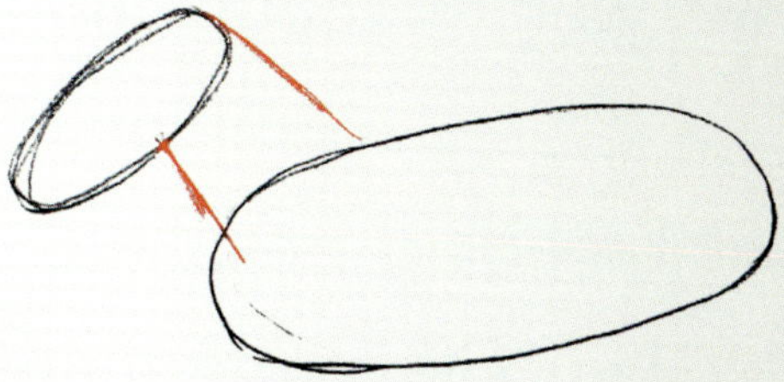

4 To make one front and one back leg, draw three circles for each. Notice the different sizes. Join each circle with two lines. Add hooves.

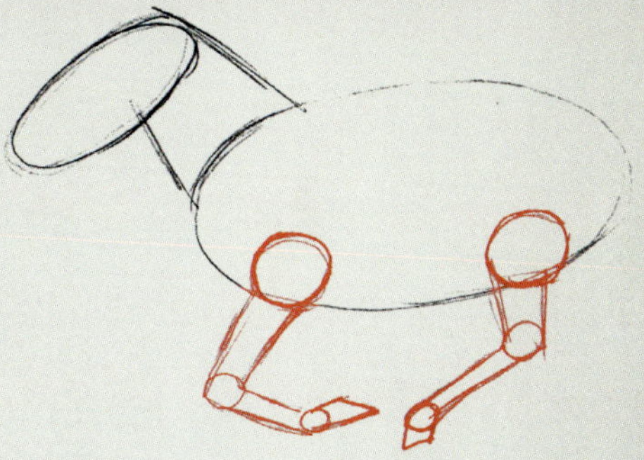

5 Now follow the same steps for the other legs. Draw circles and then connect them with lines. Remember to add the front hoof.

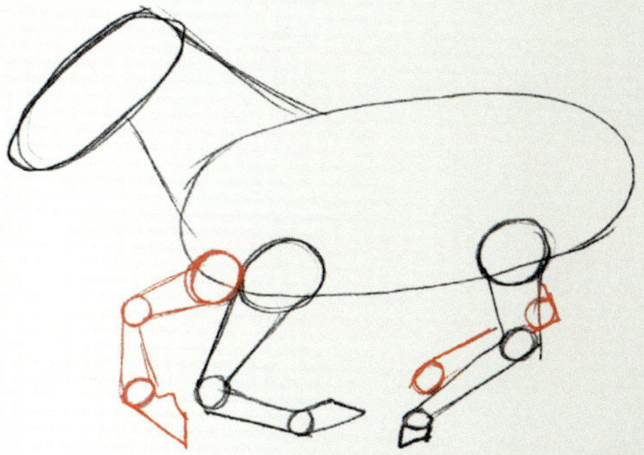

6 Next, draw the lower jaw, both ears, an eye, a nostril, and the mouth. Add the curved shapes of the tail and mane as shown. Also add the shape for the other back hoof.

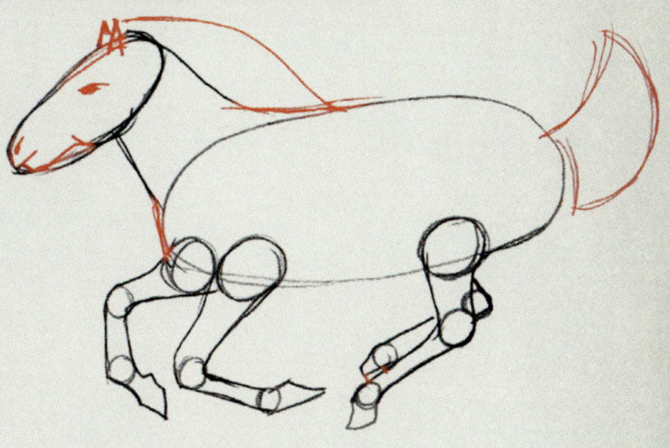

7 Erase any extra lines. Use the side of the pencil point to shade in the tail and the mane. Great job!

DRAWING THE SHIRE

Many people admire the Shire horse for its beauty. It is a draft horse, which is a type of horse that pulls loads such as wagons and plows. Draft horses are bigger and stronger than most other horses. The Shire, the world's largest horse **breed**, weighs about 1,800 pounds (816 kg)!

The Shire gets its name from its main breeding areas: the English counties of Lincolnshire, Leicestershire, Staffordshire, and Derbyshire. In the Middle Ages, Shires were used as warhorses, but today Shires are most often used to pull carts and carriages. When people take carriage rides in large cities such as New York, they may be pulled by a Shire.

The Shire is the world's largest horse breed.

1 Draw a thick oval for the body of the Shire.

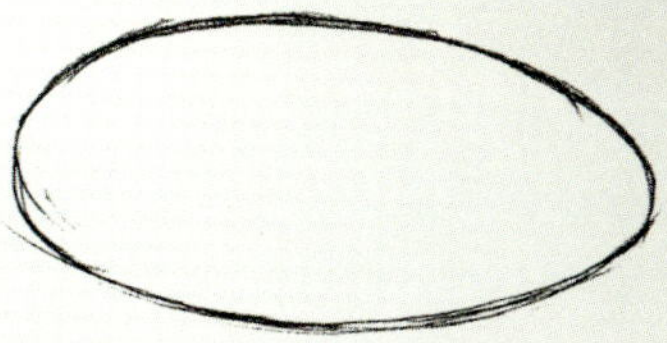

2 Draw a smaller oval for the head. Notice that it is placed above and to the right of the large oval.

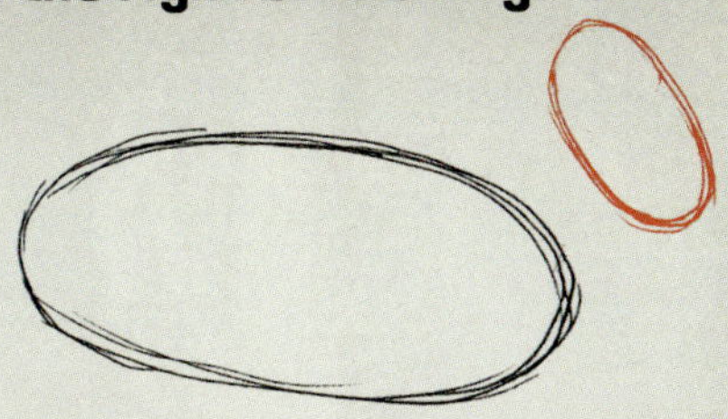

3 To add the neck, connect the ovals with two curved lines.

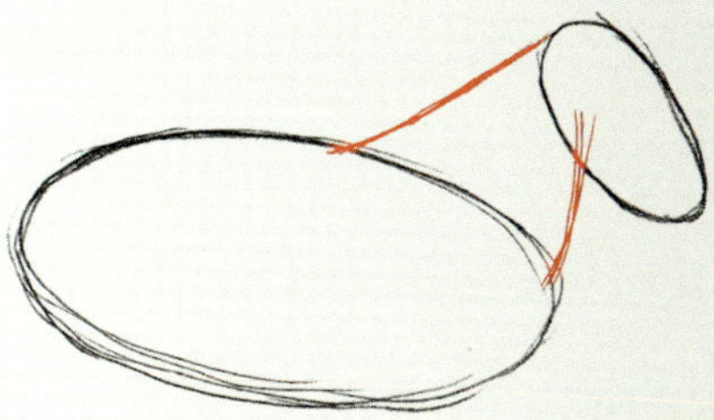

4 Now form two of the legs by first drawing three circles for each leg. Draw two lines to join the circles. Add shapes for the hooves.

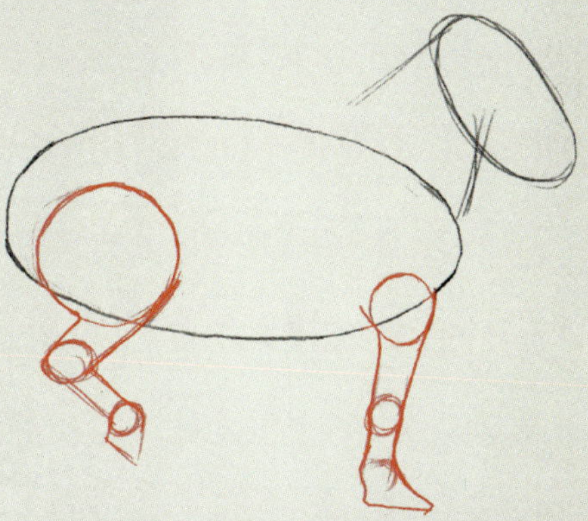

5 Next, draw the other legs and hooves. First draw circles and then add the lines to connect them.

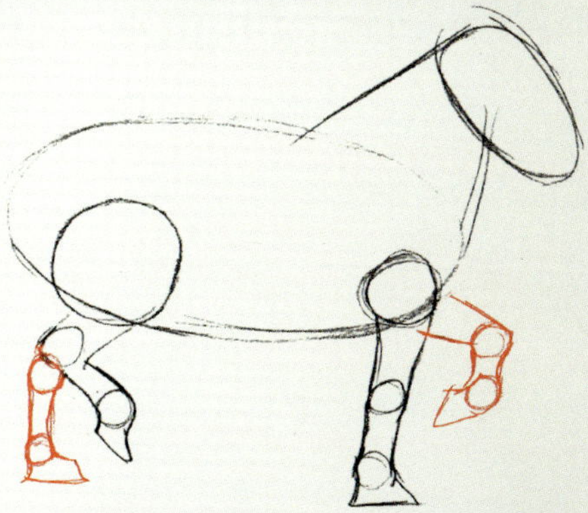

6 You're doing great! Draw the shapes of the tail and mane as shown.

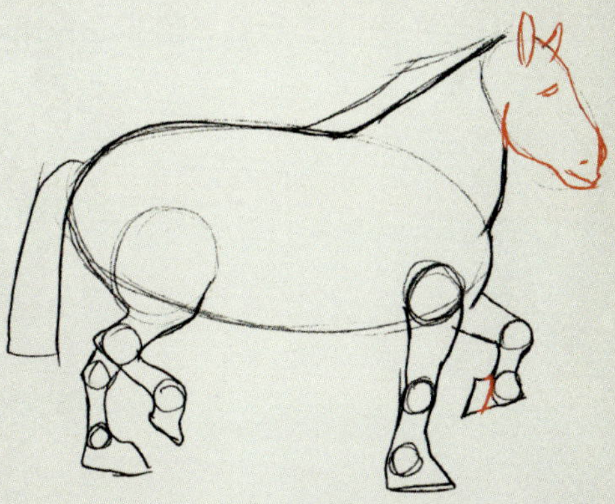

7 Add detail to the head. Draw the lower jaw, an eye, both ears, a nostril, and the mouth.

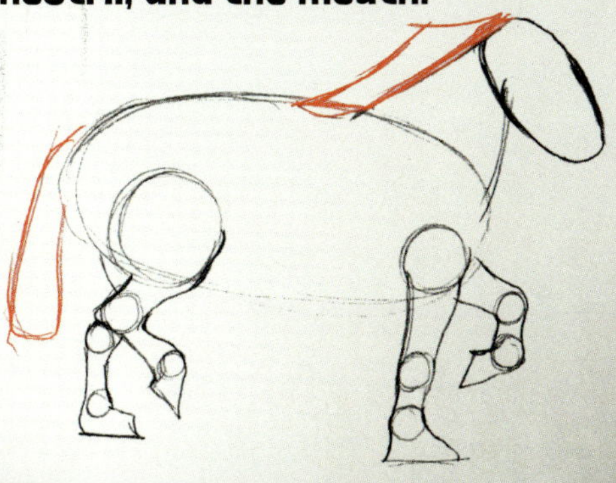

8 Erase any extra lines. Shade in the tail, mane, and feet by using the side of the pencil at a slant.

DRAWING THE QUARTER HORSE

The quarter horse got its name because it could win races that were a quarter of a mile (0.4 km) long. American **colonists** in Rhode Island and Virginia raced the quarter horse often. It is part English, part **thoroughbred**, and part Spanish. In the early 1600s, horses that had been brought from England were bred with the horses that had been brought to North America in the 1500s by the Spaniards. The result was the quarter horse.

In addition to racing, quarter horses were used on cattle ranches during roundups. Cowboys in the Old West depended on these quick and **agile** horses to control their herds of cattle.

The quarter horse is one of the most popular horses in the world.

1 Draw a beanlike shape for the body of the quarter horse.

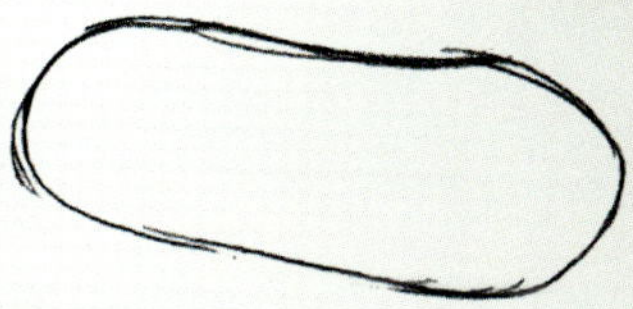

2 Add a small oval for the head. Notice how this oval is placed: a little above and to the right of the first shape.

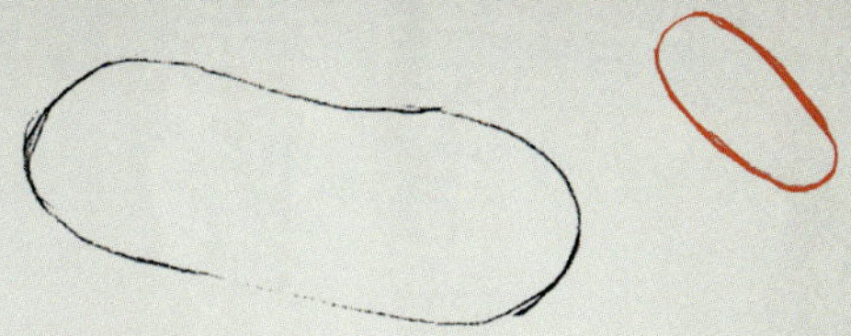

3 Now connect the two shapes with two curved lines. These lines form the neck.

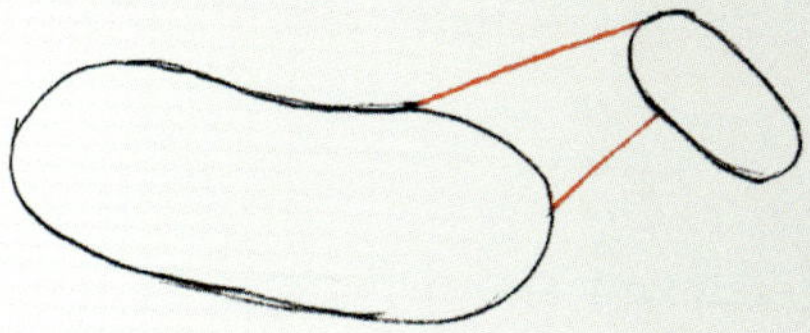

4 Next, draw three circles for the front leg and three more for the back leg. Draw lines to connect them as shown. Add the hooves.

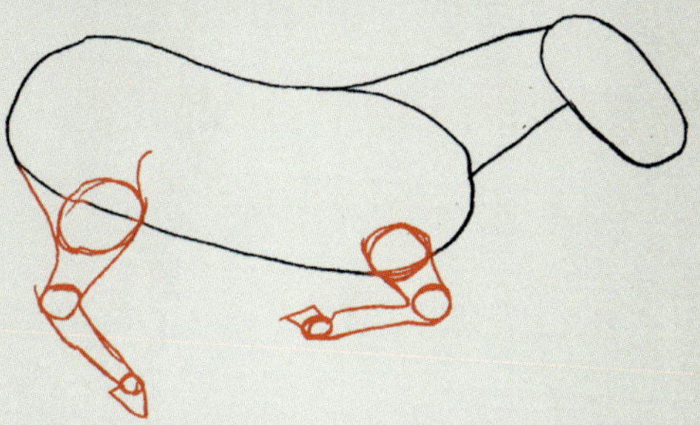

5 Now form the other legs. Draw circles and then add the lines to connect them. Draw the hooves.

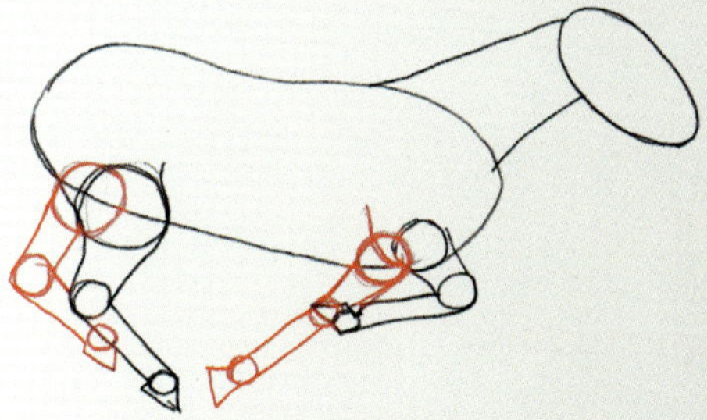

6 Next, add detail to the head by drawing the lower jaw, both ears, an eye, one nostril, and the mouth. Draw the shapes for the tail and mane as shown.

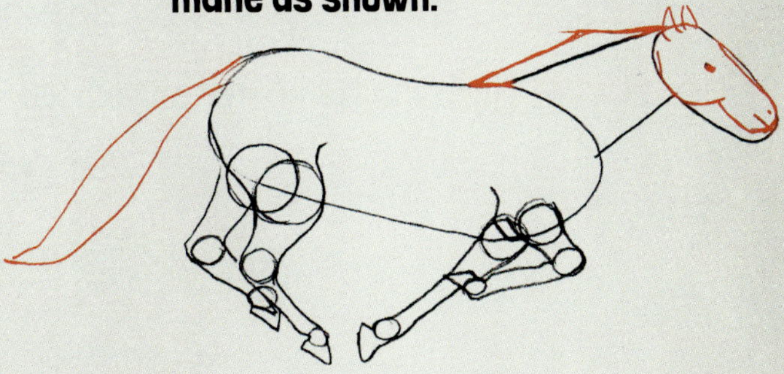

7 You're almost done! Erase any extra lines. Shade in the tail and the mane by holding the pencil with your index finger. Use the side of the pencil point at a slant by making big, wide strokes. Great job!

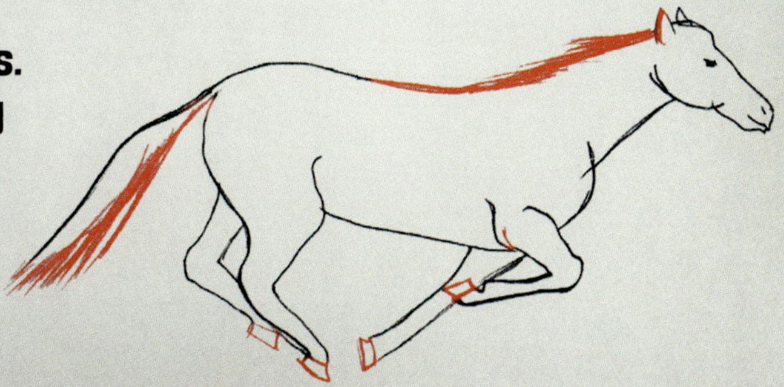

DRAWING THE THOROUGHBRED

The thoroughbred is also known as a purebred or **pedigree** horse. It is a crossbreed of several different types of horse breeds: English mares, Byerly Turk stallions, Dorley Arabian stallions, and Gondolphin Barb stallions.

The thoroughbred has an **elegant** head and neck, a long back and legs, and a broad chest. Its high energy makes it an excellent racehorse, polo pony, hunter, and jumper.

One of the most famous thoroughbreds was named Secretariat. In 1973, he won the Triple Crown, which means he won three special races that year: the Kentucky Derby, the Preakness, and the Belmont Stakes races. That is something only 12 horses in history have ever done.

Thoroughbreds are very elegant horses.

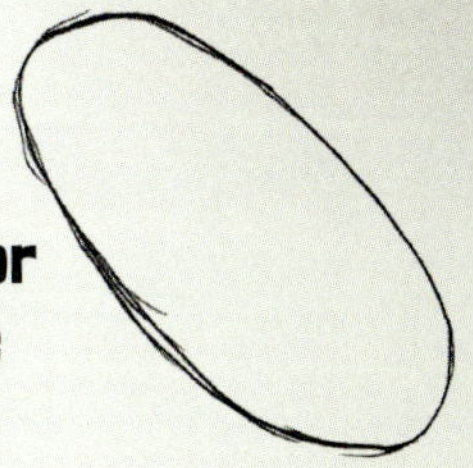

1 Draw an oval for the body of the thoroughbred. Notice how it is tilted.

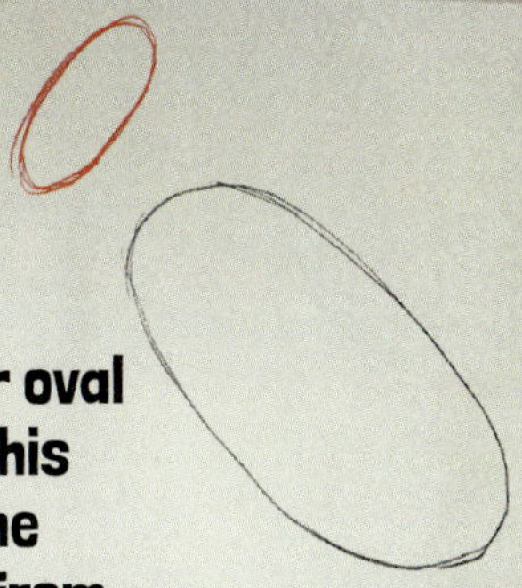

2 Draw a smaller oval for the head. This oval is tilted the opposite way from the big oval.

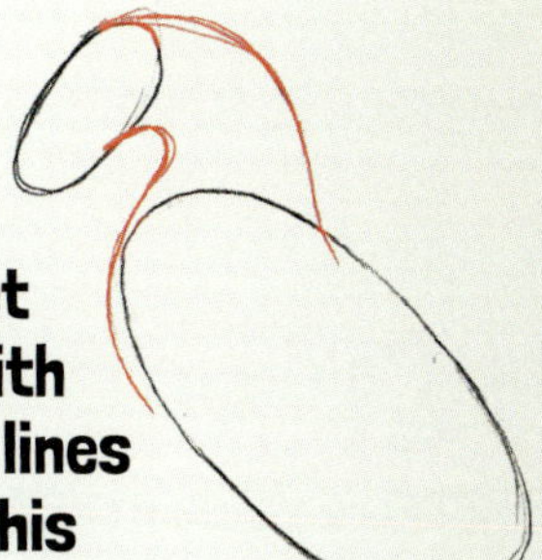

3 Now connect the ovals with two curved lines as shown. This shape forms the neck.

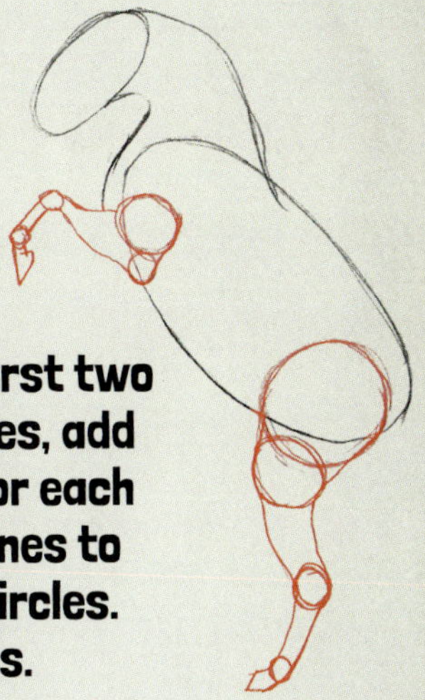

4 To draw the first two legs and hooves, add four circles for each leg. Add two lines to connect the circles. Add the hooves.

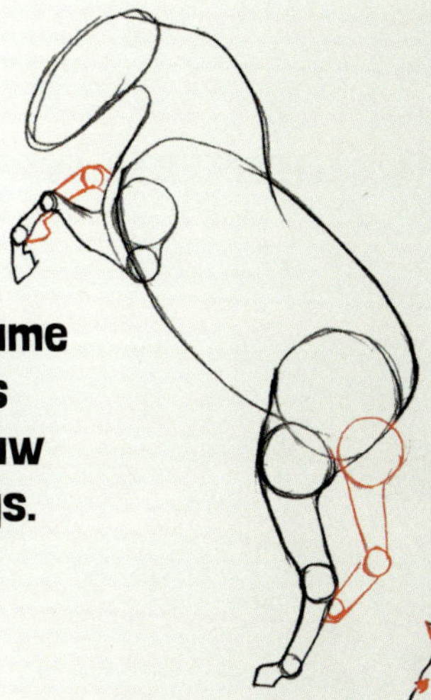

5 Follow the same directions as Step 4 to draw the other legs.

6 Excellent! Next, add some detail to the head by drawing the jaws, both ears, an eye, a nostril, and the mouth. Draw the shapes for the tail and mane as shown.

7 Erase any extra lines. Fill in the tail and the mane by holding your pencil tip on its side. Make big, wide strokes.

DRAWING THE APPALOOSA

The Appaloosa is one of the most recognizable horse breeds. Its coat has many spots and beautiful splashes of color. This type of horse is good at jumping and racing over both short and long distances.

The Appaloosa gets its name from the Palouse River, which flows in northwestern Idaho and southeastern Washington. It is believed that the breed was developed by a group of Native Americans called the Nez Percé who lived in that area. They rode Appaloosas into battle against the United States Cavalry. In 1975, the governor of Idaho signed a bill making the Appaloosa Idaho's state horse.

Appaloosas are easily recognized by their multicolored coats.

1 Draw an oval for the body of the Appaloosa.

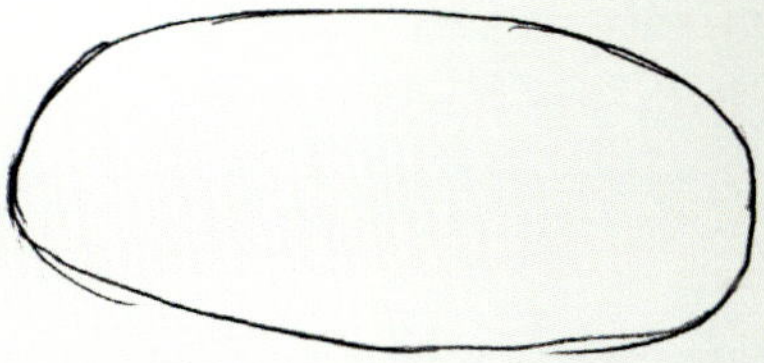

2 Next, draw a smaller oval for the head. Notice how much smaller this oval is, and where it is placed on the page compared to the first oval.

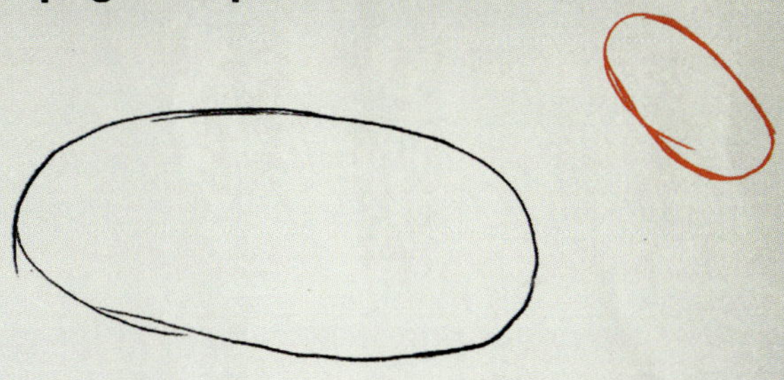

3 Now connect the ovals with two curved lines to draw the neck. Great job!

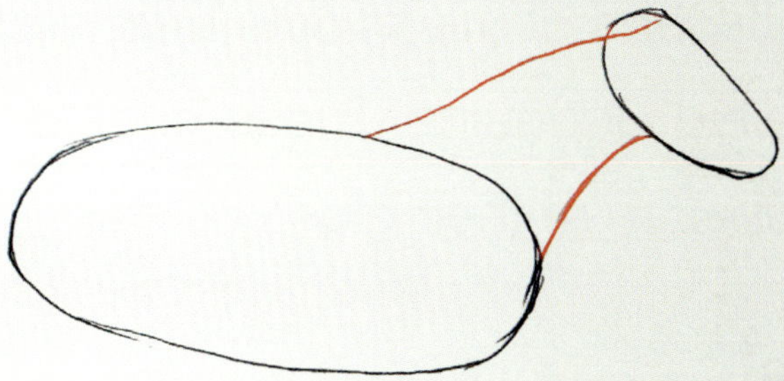

4 Now, for two of the legs, draw four circles for each. Next, add two curved lines to connect the circles. Add the hooves.

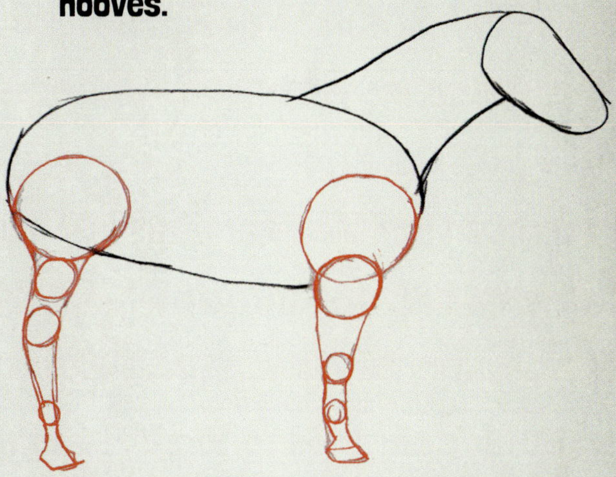

5 Follow the same steps as in Step 4 to form the other back leg. Draw circles and then add two lines to join them. Add some detail to the head by drawing in the lower jaw, the ears, an eye, and the mouth.

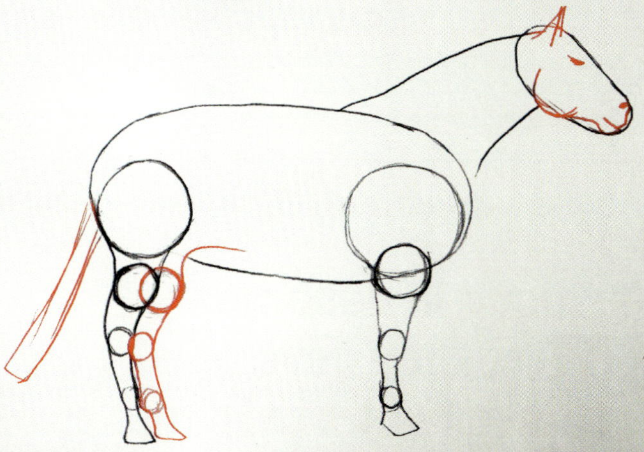

6 Erase any extra lines. Now draw the spots as shown. Add the tail and the mane by using the side of your pencil point at a slant. Great job!

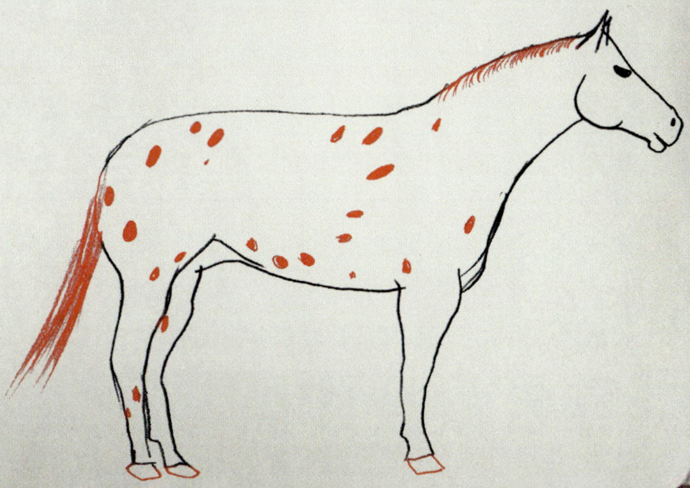

DRAWING THE ARABIAN

The Arabian is one of the oldest horse breeds in the world. It appears in ancient art, which tells us that Arabian horses probably lived as long ago as 2000 BC. These horses have been around so long that many other breeds have some Arabian in them.

The Arabian was raised in the deserts of the Middle East and North Africa by **nomadic** people called Bedouins. These people relied on their horses for survival. Because of their close contact with humans, Arabians are usually comfortable with people. They are also very **intelligent**.

During the seventh century AD, the Arabian was introduced to other countries when the religion of Islam began to spread across North Africa and into Spain.

Because Arabian horses were raised in deserts by people who were often on the move, they developed the ability to walk for a long time without stopping.

1 Draw an oval for the body of the Arabian.

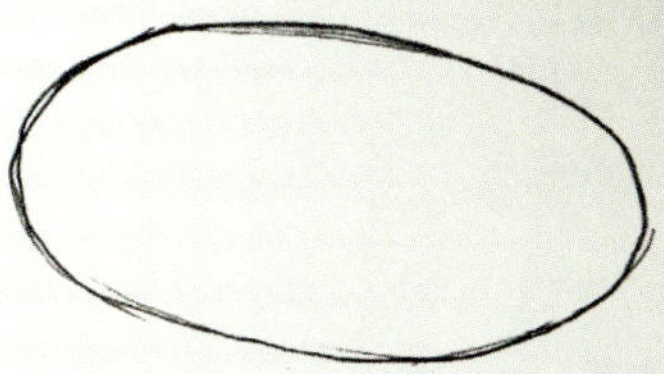

2 Draw a smaller oval at the upper right of the larger one for the head. Notice how much smaller it is and where it is placed on the page compared to the large oval.

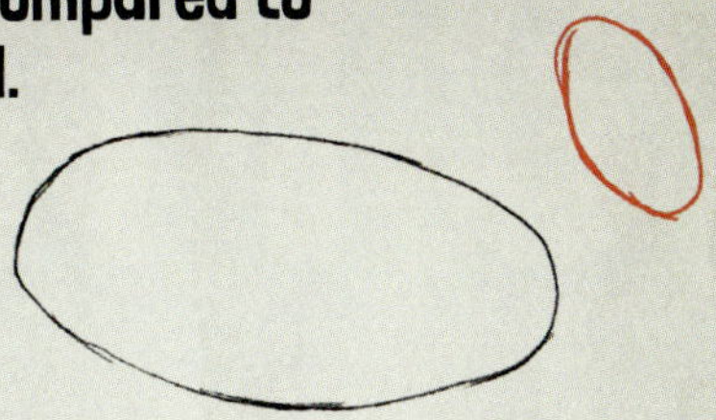

3 Now, to draw the neck, connect the ovals with two curved lines.

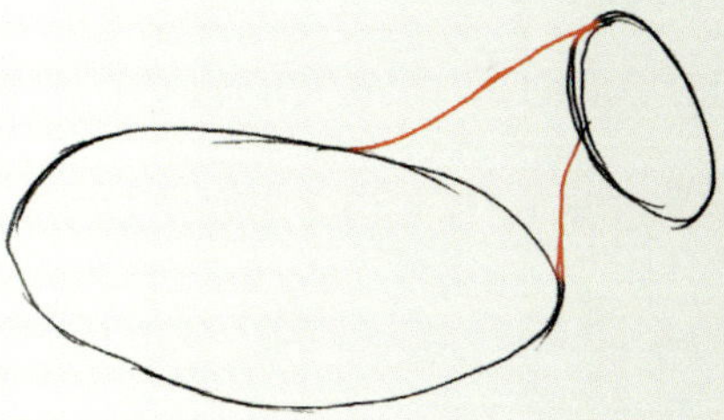

4 Draw eight circles as shown. Draw four for one front leg and four for one back leg. These circles get smaller as you go down the body. Join each set of circles with two curved lines.

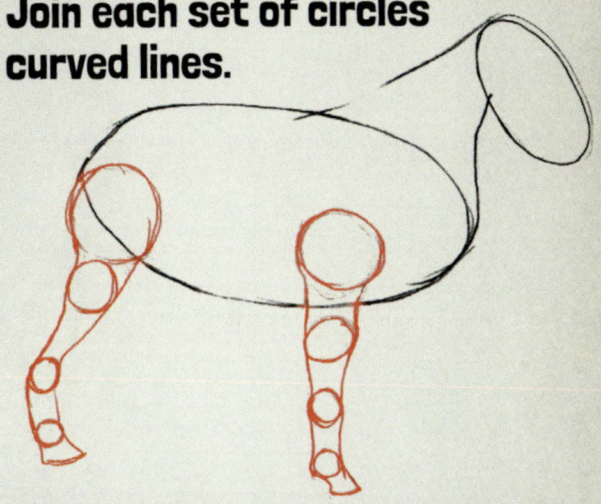

5 Now draw the same shapes for the other two legs by drawing circles and connecting them with lines as shown.

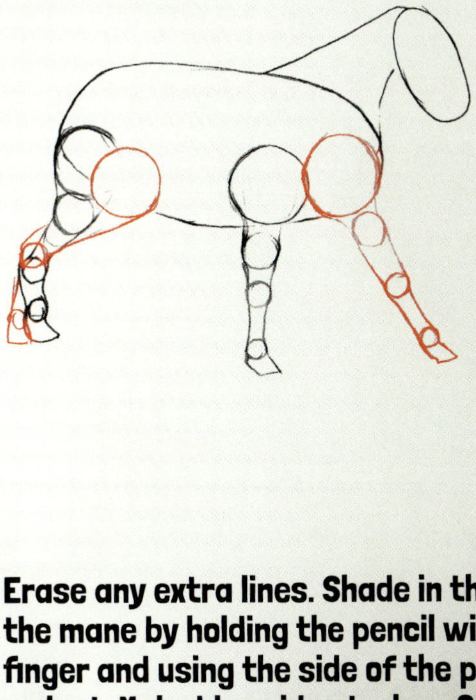

6 Next, add some detail to the head by drawing the lower jaw, the ears, an eye, a nostril, and the mouth. Now draw the basic shapes of the tail and mane as shown.

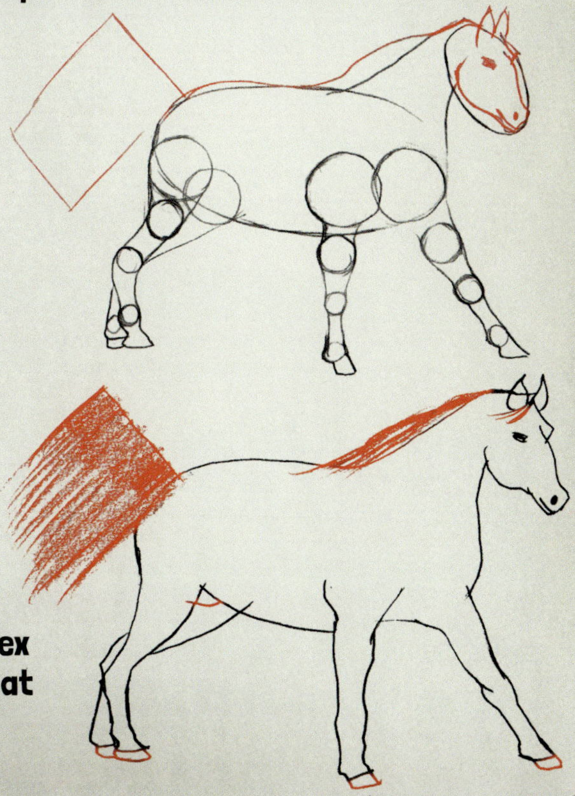

7 Erase any extra lines. Shade in the tail and the mane by holding the pencil with your index finger and using the side of the pencil point at a slant. Make big, wide strokes. Great job!

DRAWING THE SHETLAND PONY

A pony is a type of horse that is smaller than most breeds. The Shetland pony is only 11 hands high, compared to 15 hands for the average horse breed. Although it is small, it is one of the strongest horses for its size. The Shetland pony's combination of size and strength made it very useful for working in coal mines during the 19th century. Today, its small size also makes it a great horse for young riders.

Shetlands are smart and sometimes a little **stubborn**. They have thick coats and manes because they were raised in the Shetland Islands off the northern coast of Scotland, where it is often cold and rainy.

Shetland ponies' thick fur keeps them warm in cold climates.

1 Draw an oval for the body of the Shetland.

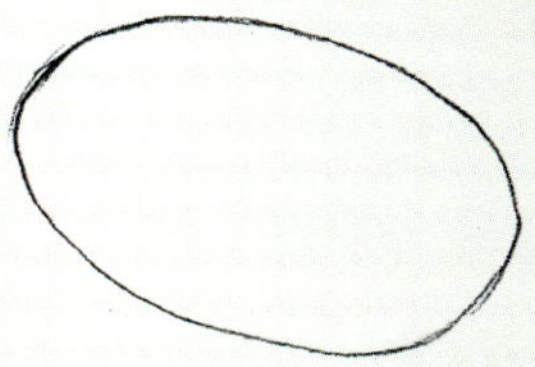

2 Draw a smaller oval for the head. Notice that it is placed above and to the right of the first oval.

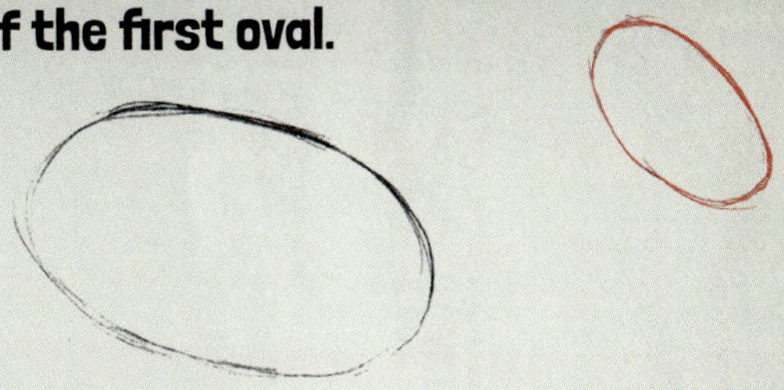

3 Now connect the ovals with two curved lines to draw the neck.

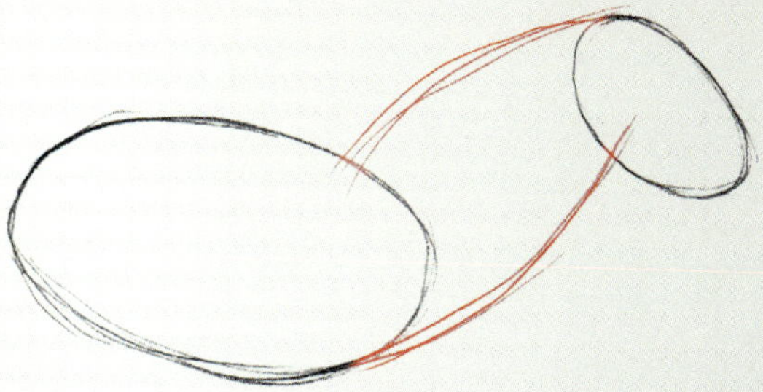

4 Add two of the legs by first drawing three circles for each leg. Draw two sets of curved lines as shown to join the circles. Add the hooves.

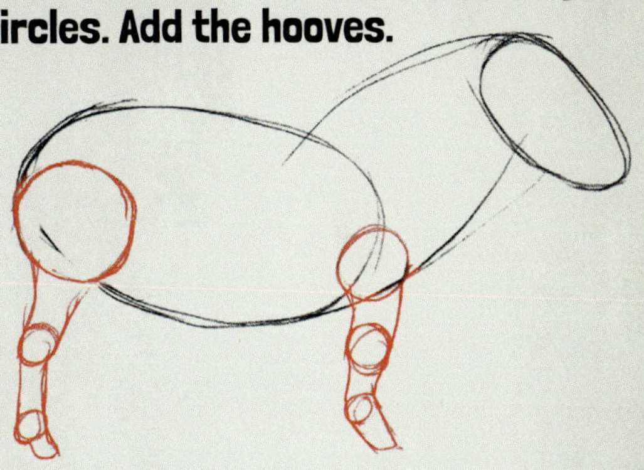

5 Now follow the directions in Step 4 for the other legs. Draw the circles first and then add the lines to join them. Add the two hooves.

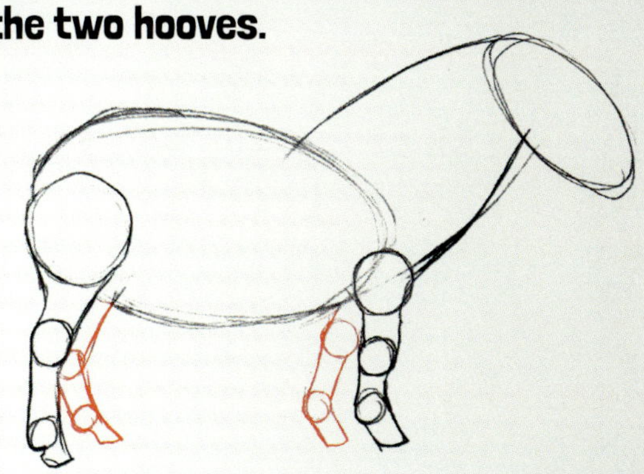

6 Now draw the shapes of the tail and mane as shown.

7 Erase any extra lines. Add the small, curved line for the mouth. Shade in the tail and the mane by holding your pencil on its side at a slant. Make big, wide strokes. Well done!

DRAWING TERMS

There are some words and shapes you will need to know to draw horses.

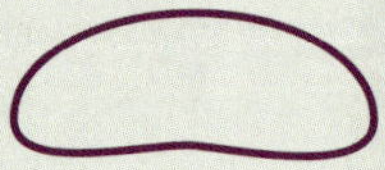 **beanlike shape**

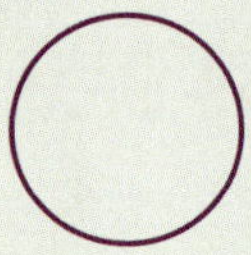 **circle**

 **curved line**

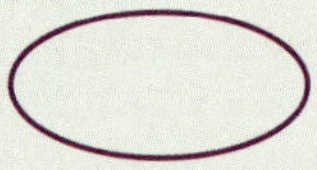 **oval**

 **shade**

GLOSSARY

adapted: Changed to suit a situation or purpose.

agile: Able to move quickly yet easily and gracefully.

breed: A group of animals that look very much alike and have the same kind of relatives.

colonists: People who live in a colony, a place where they are still ruled by the leaders and laws of their old country.

conquistadores: Spanish explorers who tried to take over Mexico by force in the 1500s.

crossbred: When two or more kinds of breeds with the same species are crossed.

domesticated: Tamed by humans.

elegant: Being graceful or beautiful.

intelligent: Having the ability to learn and understand information.

nomadic: Traveling from place to place rather than settling down in one area.

pedigree: Referring to an impressive family history.

species: A group of living things that have certain basic things in common.

stagecoaches: Horse-drawn carriages that carried passengers and mail to certain stops on a regular schedule.

stubborn: Wanting to have one's own way, or being difficult.

thoroughbred: An animal that has been bred to have a clean, respected bloodline.

INDEX

A
Appaloosa, 16, 17
Arabian, 18, 19

B
Bedouins, 18
Belmont Stakes, 14

K
Kentucky Derby, 14

M
Mongolia, 6
mustang, 8, 9

N
Nez Percé, 16

P
Palouse River, 16
Preakness, 14
Prezewalski, Nikolai, 6
Przewalski's horse, 4, 6, 8

Q
quarter horse, 12, 13

S
Shetland pony, 20, 21
Shire, 10, 11

T
thoroughbred, 14, 15
Triple Crown, 14

WEBSITES

Due to the changing nature of Internet links, PowerKids Press has developed an online list of websites related to the subject of this book. This site is updated regularly. Please use this link to access the list: www.powerkidslinks.com/ltd/horses